crazy Clay CREATURES

maureen carlson

IMPACT
CINCINNATI, OHIO
www.impact-books.com

Contents

1 SHAPE MONSTERS

2 NOT-QUITE-SO-ORDINARY BEASTS

3 CREATURES FROM THE DUMP

4 THINGS THAT WALK ON TWO LEGS

5 DINOSAURS AND DRAGONS

Note for Adults

The clay that is used for the projects in this book is a super soft, lightweight, air dry clay. There are many brands on the market, including, among others, Cloud Clay, Creatology Air Dry Clay and Model Magic. These clays come in a variety of colors and they're fun to play with, even for adults!

The packages may vary in consistency depending on the brand and whether or not the package is air tight. Since the clay begins to dry upon contact with air, it is important to keep the clay protected in airtight containers or bags. Generally it dries to the touch in 24 hours. If the clay is too soft, leave it exposed to air until it starts to dry a bit.

Usually the clay does not stick to hands, though it sticks very easily to itself. Provide your child with a suitable work area as some of the colors may stain hands or work surfaces. Washing with soap and water will remove most stains. Oven-baked polymer clay, kiln-fired clays and heavier, wetter air dry clays are not appropriate for the projects in this book.

using super lightweight air dry clay

Opening a package of clay is a bit like stepping through a door into a grand adventure. What you see may at first seem quite ordinary, but stay with it a bit and the possibilities may surprise you. You can transform colorful air dry clay into things you've seen and those you've only imagined. This book is full of tips, tricks and ideas to help you do just that.

Use the Right Clay
Does the clay that you are using feel light, like a marshmallow? Are the words *Air Dry* printed somewhere on the package? If so, then you probably have clay that will work for the projects in this book.

Keep It Separated!
If you want one piece of clay to stick to another, just touch them together. It's that easy. If you don't want them to stick, keep the pieces separated. Don't believe me? Try it. You'll see!

Mix It Up
Create striped clay by twisting two or more colors together. Make solid colors by twisting the colors together, then roll and fold, then twist again. The new color you get might surprise you!

Prop It

Help your creations keep their shape by propping them up until they are completely dry. This won't matter for some pieces, but an arm that you want to stay up in the air or those wings that are posed for lift-off will droop if not propped in place.

Keep It Covered

Clay that is dried out doesn't stick to itself very well. And it doesn't roll into a smooth ball or shape. To keep it fresh, store it in an airtight container or bag. Seal the container every time you use the clay. I know, it's a real bother, but your clay will last longer and you'll be able to make more stuff.

Put Different Colors in a Large Plastic Bag

Put all of the colors that you'll use for a project into one large gallon-sized bag. Keep colors separate by placing them in different corners of the bag. Flatten the bag to press out the air, then fold over the top if you'll be using it right away. Remember to tightly close the bag when you're done with the project so that you can use the clay another time.

Revive Dried-Out Clay

If your clay dries out, try folding and twisting it to see if it becomes workable. Still too dry? Place it in a plastic bag and sprinkle just a little bit of water on it. Too much water will make it very sticky. Leave it in the bag for a few minutes, then twist and mix it to see if it's workable again. If your clay is very dry, you may have to add more water and let it rest even longer. Completely dried out clay cannot usually be revived, so remember to keep it covered!

tools you can use

Find a can or box to use for storing your tools. That way, they'll be ready whenever you feel like making something. Most anything can be used as a tool, but here are some things that you might want to put in your toolbox.

FILL YOUR TOOLBOX

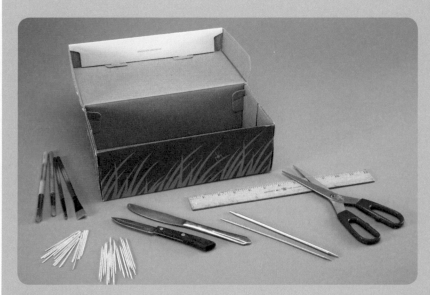

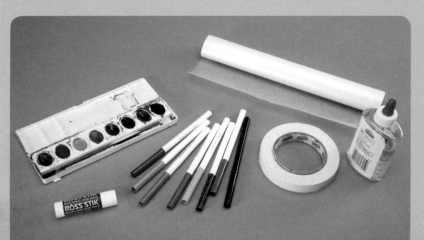

Barbecue Skewers

Craft sticks

Dull knife

Flat and round toothpicks

Glue that dries clear

Glue stick

Knitting needles

Masking tape

Paintbrushes

Paper clips

Ruler

Scissors

Straws

String

Twisty ties

Watercolor markers

Watercolor paint

Wax paper

Yarn

recycled art supplies

Not all art supplies need to be purchased. Toilet and paper towel tubes, boxes and scrap paper can be rescued from the trash bin. Watch for small jars and cans in the trash and save them to use as handy containers. Deli cartons and straws can be turned into terrific tools. Be sure that the cans have no sharp edges. Wash everything well before storing with your art supplies.

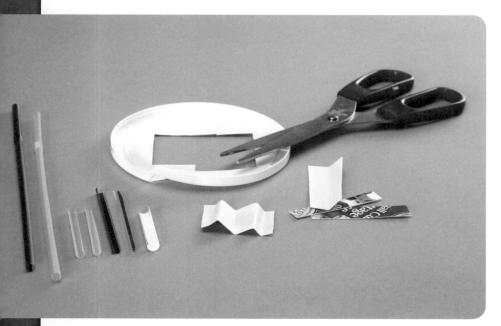

Turn straws and deli cartons into terrific tools for making mouths, eyelids, fingernails and lines. Small pieces can also be used as cutting tools. To form the straw tools, cut a straw into short sections, then cut each section in half lengthwise. Trim some pieces to create a narrow half-circle, and some to make wider ones. To use the deli cartons, cut them into short strips, then bend the strips to create U, V or W shapes.

Look around the floor of your room or under your bed. Do you see anything there that could be combined with air dry clay? Bits of this and that from broken toys or discarded equipment just might become treasures when used in an art project. See what you can find.

make an eyeball

You can use a plain black clay ball as an eyeball, but you can make it more interesting if you start with a white or colored ball and then add a black dot for the pupil. Or, start with a large ball, add a colored clay ball and keep adding details.

There isn't a right or a wrong way. It depends on how you're using the eyes. You get to decide how much detail you want to add. It makes a difference if the eyeballs are really big or very tiny.

Make a stash of eyes in different sizes and colors to let harden so they're ready to use for the projects ahead!

Rolling a ball seems simple enough. Just rotate your hands in a circle as you press lightly against the clay.

Basic Eye

For a simple eye, roll one white ball and one black one. Flatten the black ball and press to the center of the white one. Notice how much bigger the black ball gets when it's flattened.

Add Color

Make the eyeball look more realistic by adding a colored iris before you press the pupil in place. Remember that a ball gets bigger when you flatten it, so start with a tiny ball for the iris and an even tinier one for the pupil.

Detailed Eye

For a really detailed eye, add a tiny white ball to show the reflection of light. Add it to the line between the color and the black, putting it in the same place on each eye, either on top, to the right or to the left. This white highlight makes your character seem more alive. Tip: If the tiny white dot is too hard to pick up with your fingers, use a tooth-pick to pick it up and position it on the eye.

But if you press too lightly as you roll, or if the clay is too dry, you won't get the wrinkles out. If you press too hard, you may get a disk or football shape.

ball monsters with teeth

Make a Stash of Teeth

It's easy to squish soft teeth when you're trying to put them in place. Teeth that are a bit hard will be easier to use. Before you start your projects, take some time to make a pile of teeth in different sizes, then let them harden for an hour or two, or overnight if you can wait! Once they're really dry, you can pile them into a little box. They'll keep until you're ready to use them.

Add pointy teeth to a simple ball shape, then add eyes. Just like that you've created a monster. Once you've made one ball monster, quickly roll another ball and add really big eyes to that one. Now do something more to it. Can you change the shape of the mouth or add a nose? Keep making balls and then changing them, one thing at a time. Before long you'll have a whole troop of monsters. Or would you call them a horde?

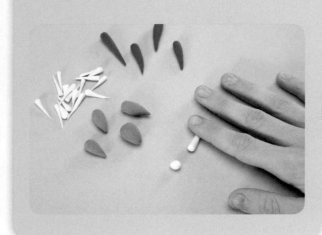

1 MAKE TEETH
Begin by rolling 8 small white balls. Turn into cones by rolling along one side of the ball. Roll just a bit and you'll have an egg shape. Keep rolling and you'll turn it into a cone or dagger, perfect for monster teeth!

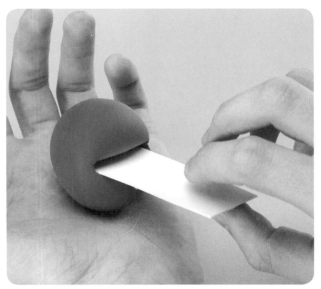

2 ROLL A BALL

The head begins as a ball shape. Use a plastic tool or a knife to cut in the mouth. Rock the tool up and down to open the mouth wider.

3 ADD THE TEETH

Press in teeth and close the mouth.

4 ADD EYES

To make the monster seem almost alive, add a small black ball for the pupil. Note that ball shapes get bigger when you flatten them! The final touch is the tiny white highlight which mimics a reflection of light. The highlight goes on the same side of each eye. A toothpick may make it easier to pick up and place these tiny balls. Be sure and flatten them a bit so that they stay in place.

5 MAKE AN EYELID

To make an eyelid, make a small ball, then flatten it. Cut the flattened clay circle in half. Pick up one half, curve it a bit and place it over the eye. Press down slightly.

square monsters with horns

Is there room for some square monsters in the monster horde?

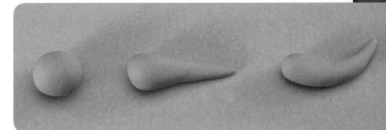

1 MAKE A SQUARE
Start with a ball shape. Press the ball with a flat object like a block. Turn and press again. Repeat until all six sides are flat.

2 CREATE HORNS
To make horns, use the same technique you learned for making ball monster teeth, but start with bigger balls of clay. Curve the horns, then set them aside to dry. Press in place.

Different Kinds of Mouths

Each tool that you use to make the mouth will create a different shape. Round, smooth knitting needles make mouths that look like they're singing or howling. Pushing the tool in deep will create a different look than if you make a shallow hole. Experiment with your tools to see how many kinds of mouths you can make.

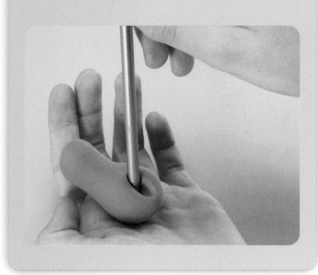

3 ADD FEATURES
Add eyeballs and use a plastic tool to cut the mouth. Use a toothpick to pull down the corner so he's frowning.

drumstick monsters with ears

You're rolling right along now! Ready for another shape? Let's try a drumstick!

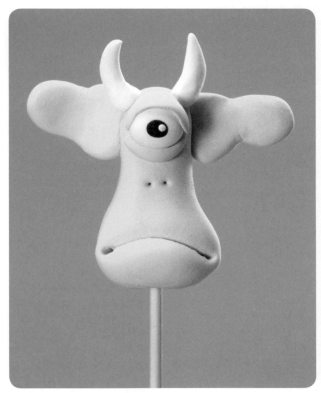

1 MAKE A DRUMSTICK

Make a ball, then roll your finger along the middle of the ball, pressing lightly as you go. Press too hard and you'll flatten the drumstick. Make one larger drumstick for the head and two smaller ones for the ears.

2 CREATE THE EARS.

Flatten the two smaller drumsticks and press to the head.

3 ADD FEATURES

Cut in the mouth. Add whatever features you imagine it to have.

troop of egg monsters

Your own head is shaped a bit like an egg. Does that mean that you're an egg monster or you just act like one? Or maybe you're just an egghead?

You learned to make egg shapes when you made teeth, but larger egg shapes are easier to make if you use your whole hand. Notice that some of the noses are just little eggs!

1 MAKE AN EGG
Place the ball between your two hands with the bottom sides of your hands touching. Slide your hands back and forth so that the bottom part of the ball starts to get smaller and pointed. Keep your hands in a V shape and don't let your thumbs touch. The closer together your hands get, the skinnier the egg becomes.

Another way to make an egg shape is to lay a ball on the table, then place your hand on top of it in a tilted position. Slide your tilted hand back and forth over the ball. Keep rolling and sliding your hand so the clay changes into an egg, then a teardrop and then a carrot.

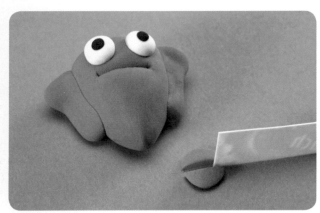

2 ADD MOUTHS, EYES AND EARS.
Flatten drumsticks to create the ears. Flatten balls and cut in half for the eyelids. Cut the mouth with a plastic tool.

3 CREATE THE NOSE
You can make another small egg or ball shape to fit your shape monster's personality.

4 CHANGE IT UP
You can add teeth, horns and other features for each member of this wild troop.

cone and football monsters

Here come the cone and football monsters. Is there room for them in your lineup? Activate your imagination! How many different monsters can you make using the same or similar shapes?

1 **MAKE A FOOTBALL**
Roll both ends of an egg into a point and it will turn into a football.

2 Use your recycled plastic tools in creative ways. This mouth was made using a bent piece of plastic from a deli carton. Pinch the sides of the tool as you press it in and you'll change the shape that it makes.

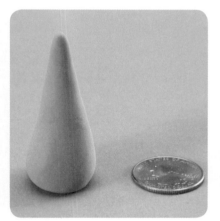

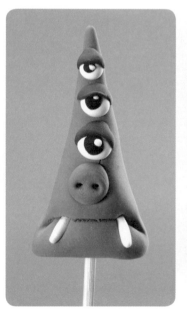

3 Creating a cone is just like creating an egg, but roll it longer to make it more pointed. Press down on the wide part to create a flat bottom.

4 Create an entire team of characters by adding teeth or varying the width of the eyes.

off with their heads!

Mix and match for an endless parade of monsters. The heads and bodies for this cast of characters were made separately, then allowed to dry. This way they won't stick together. You can take them on and off and on and off. Well, you get it!

These characters are made with shapes that you've already learned to make. You might recognize some of the heads from past projects. Experiment with using twigs for arms and toothpicks or skewers to hold the heads.

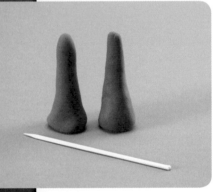

1 For the legs, make two cone shapes.

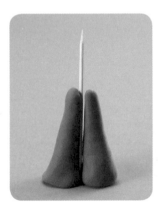

2 To keep your guy from wobbling, press a stick against one leg, then sandwich legs together with the stick in the middle.

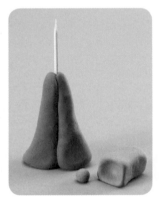

3 For the body, make a square shape. Press a shallow hole into the bottom of the square. Press the body over the legs, fitting them into the hole.

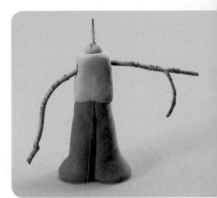

4 Add a ball for the neck and sticks for the arms. Press a toothpick into the neck, leaving part sticking out. Where's his head?

VARIATIONS

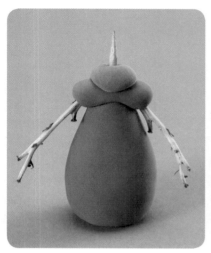

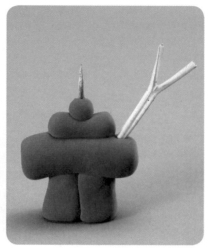

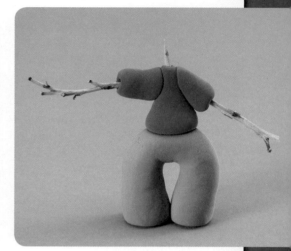

An egg creates a dress shape for a female monster!

Four ropes and a ball are the only shapes you need to make this body.

Use two short ropes and a cone to create a T-shirt. Stick twigs in for arms. A larger rope bent in half creates a set of legs.

big-tooth, the spot-bellied fish

MATERIALS

Yellow, orange, white and black clay

Hot pink and green watercolor markers

String • Paper clip

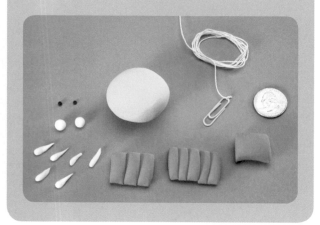

Flying fish. Are there REALLY flying fish? Well, this one flies through the air…or at least swings in the breeze. Hang him up where he can see what's going on. He looks a little afraid, doesn't he?

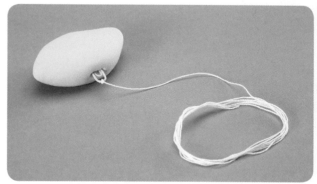

1 CREATE THE BODY
Make football shape from yellow clay. Flatten slightly. Tie a string to a paper clip and press it into the top of fish. Completely bury it so that only the string shows.

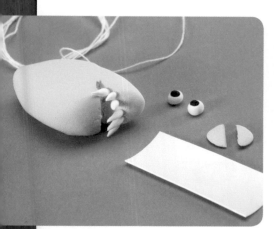

2 FORM THE MOUTH AND EYES
Use a plastic tool to open the mouth really wide. Press in 6 pre-made teeth. Close the mouth and add eyes.

If you plan on using markers or paint, you'll get brighter colors if you use white clay for the parts you'll paint.

3 MAKE THE TAIL
Roll the tail fin piece into a ball and then into a football shape. Flatten slightly, then press in place. Roll the rest of the fin pieces into balls and then into egg shapes. Flatten and press in place. There are 3 side fins on the back, too. Use a toothpick to press lines in fins.

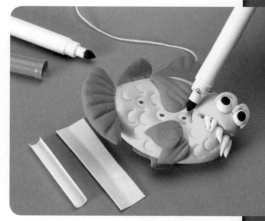

4 FORM THE SCALES
Use a straw to press scale marks all over your fish. Use a bent plastic tool to create the gill. Let dry overnight, then use some markers to add spots into the middle of each scale.

spike, the sharp-horned snake

Next time you go for a walk outside, see if you can find a stick that would be just the right shape to use as a snake perch. Then make Spike to help guard your room. When you color him, do you want to use the colors of a real snake or do you like the fantasy colors that are used here on Spike? You get to choose.

MATERIALS

White, black and yellow clay

Watercolor paint • Watercolor markers

Stick • Straw

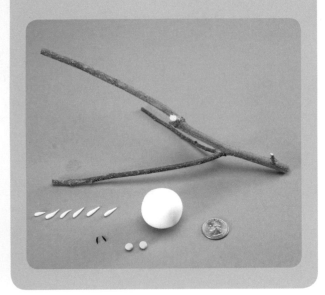

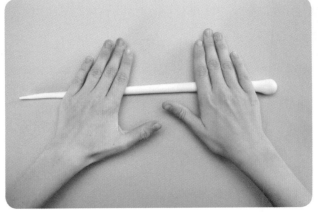

1 MAKE A CLAY ROPE
Roll white clay into a ball and then into a long tapered rope. Keep the rope smooth by stretching it as you roll. Do this by slowly moving your hands apart at the same time as you roll the clay.

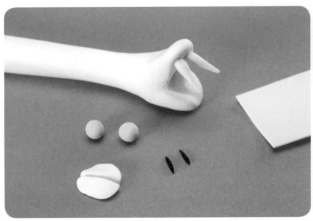

2 CREATE THE HEAD
Flatten the head end slightly and reshape snout. Cut in the mouth using the plastic tool. Add teeth, eyes and eyelids.

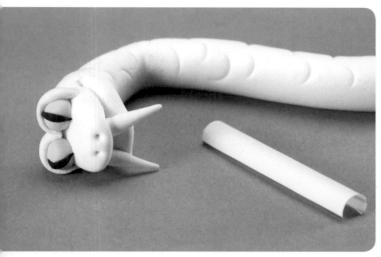

3 ADD TEXTURE
Add texture by pressing the surface with the round end of a straw. Use a toothpick to create holes for the nose.

4 CREATE THE CURVES
Wrap snake loosely around a stick. You'll want to be able to remove it after it is dry so that you can paint it. You can add spikes to the head and balls to the tail for a rattle. Let it harden until very firm, at least overnight.

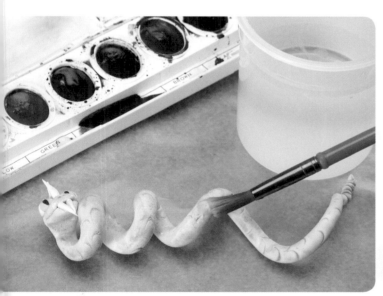

5 ADD COLOR
Make sure you have an old paper bag or newspaper to protect your table from paint. Use watercolor to paint your snake, starting with the lightest colors. Let dry.

6 ADD LINES AND DOTS
Use watercolor markers to create your patterns. If you want the lines to be more blurry, brush lightly with a wet brush. CAUTION! Remember that too much water will make the clay sticky, and there's nothing quite so unmanageable as a sticky spiked snake!

brute the blue, a long-beaked bird

Is Brute the Blue hungry or is he singing? Projects are always more fun if you tell a story for your clay creations. Decide what Brute the Blue is doing, then add a worm or a fish or, perhaps, nothing at all to his beak. Maybe this is the beast that Big-Tooth, the Spot-Bellied Fish is afraid of!

MATERIALS

Watercolor markers • Watercolor paints

6 blue twisty ties • Clay: blue, white, black

Stick

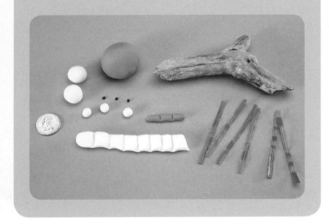

1 CREATE THE BODY
Roll the body into an egg shape, then lean the body against a stick so the egg sits up. For each leg, twist three ties together, leaving the ends separated for toes.

Remove body from stick. Press legs into Brute's belly. Press the back against stick and shape body to give a slight curve towards tail.

2 CREATE THE BEAK
Roll two beak pieces into cone shapes, then press cones around end of paintbrush handle to flatten them and form them into beak shapes.

Press beak, still on the handle, into place on head. Roll handle to release beak from handle. Tip: If you leave the handle in place for a little bit to let the beak harden, it will keep its shape better when the handle is removed.

3 MAKE THE EYEBALLS

Make 3 eyeballs. Set one aside, press two in place. Cut 6 eyelids and layer 2 to 3 overlapping eyelids over the back of each eyeball.

4 ADD FEATHERS

Roll white pieces into balls, then eggs. Flatten each, then press in lines with a toothpick to make feathers. Press feathers in place using 3 for tail, 2 for each wing and one on top of the head. Add a third eye with an eyelid to the feather on top.

5 ADD COLOR

Let it dry until firm. Add color with paints and markers. Use what you learned about paints when you created Spike the Snake.

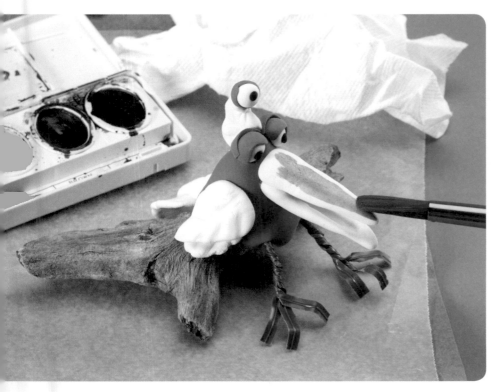

quick-tongue sal, the amphibian

Is Sal a frog or a toad? Does his species exist or does he live only in your imagination? You can turn this project into many different kinds of amphibians by adding different spikes or bumps and using different colors of clay and markers. You could even create a whole swamp full, errrr… room full of amphibians.

MATERIALS

Green, yellow, red and blue clay

Purple and orange watercolor markers

Toothpick

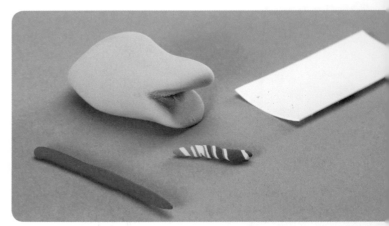

1 FORM THE BODY

Roll body ball into a short drumstick shape. Press and roll larger end into a short point for the tail. Flatten the head end slightly.

2 MAKE THE MOUTH

Cut in the mouth using a plastic tool. Make a worm by twisting together tiny ropes of red, yellow and blue clay. For the tongue, roll red clay into a long rope. Place the worm on the end of the tongue and roll the tongue around the worm. Place tongue in mouth and close.

3 FINISH THE FACE

Poke in two holes for the nose. Add yellow eyeballs. To make long pupils, press a short black rope across each eye, then add a black ball in the middle. Add white highlights. Add half-circles to make the eyelids.

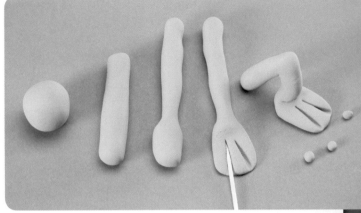

4 MAKE THE LEGS

Make legs, beginning by rolling each into a ball, then a rope. Notice that the front legs are a lot smaller than the powerful back legs. Flatten one end of each for the foot. Press in 3 lines to make toes. Press a tiny ball at the end of each toe. Bend once at elbows and knees and once at wrist and ankle. (Do amphibians have wrists and ankles?!!!)

5 ADD THE LEGS TO THE BODY

Press legs in place. Add green balls of clay at knees and elbows.

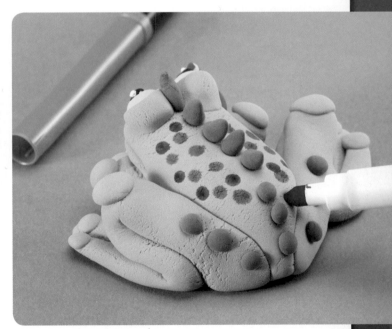

6 FINISH THE DETAILS

Add 5 purple clay spikes along the back and 3 purple balls along each leg and tail. Let dry. Use watercolor markers to add orange to the toes and orange and purple dots to the back.

If you have trouble getting the spikes to stick, you can use a small bit of washable glue.

big o, the freckled orangutan

Create Big O and imagine that you're swinging through the trees with the Orangutan team. Looks like Big O just struck out.

In this project you'll create simple hands and feet. You'll be making hands and feet again for later projects. If you need more help with how to do it, go to **Things That Walk on Two Legs**.

MATERIALS

Orange, brown, white and purple clay

Brown watercolor marker

Stick

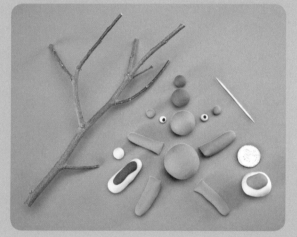

Mixing Colors

When mixing colors, start with the lightest color. Add just a bit of the darker colors to the lighter one. Mix it in, then add more of the darker colors if you like. Sometimes I've ended up with a huge ball of a mixed color, way more than I wanted, because it got too dark and I had to keep adding more white to it until I got the color that I wanted.

1 FORM THE BODY

Begin Big O with an egg shape. Position the body on stick. Roll legs and arms into short ropes. Bend ropes at elbows and knees, then press them to the body.

2 MAKE THE BALL AND BAT

Form a plain white ball. Mix brown with white to get a wood color. Form a tapered rope and place a flattened ball at the end. Let it harden or he won't be able to hold it.

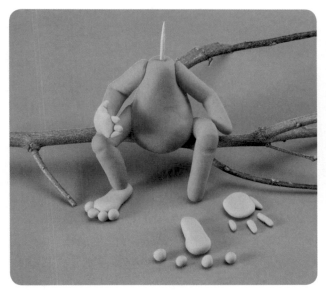

3 CREATE HANDS AND FEET

Mix a bit of orange with white clay for his lighter hands, feet and face. Flatten a drumstick shape for each foot. Flatten a square for each hand. Roll eight small balls for toes and eight small ropes for fingers. Place the toes at the end of the foot; the thumb at the base of the hand and the rest of the fingers at the end.

Bend the hand so it will be ready to hold the bat.

4 ADD THE FACE

Make an egg to create his head, small part up. Make another egg for his muzzle and a flattened rectangle for the lighter color around the eyes. For his ears, create a flattened ball and push onto his head.

Add the eye mask first, then flatten the egg for his mouth and cheeks and add to the middle of his face.

Cut in his mouth with a plastic tool and add toothpick marks at side of his mouth. Add his eyeballs. Push them toward the middle slightly to create the bridge of the nose.

Add his head to his body.

5 ADD THE EYEBROWS AND NOSE

Put a rope ring around each eye. Add a little ball and press with a toothpick to form the nose and nostrils. Make two small ropes for eyebrows. Tilt the eyerows toward his nose to make him look angry.

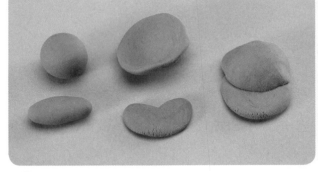

6 FORM THE HAT

Use your thumb to hollow out the inside of a ball to make a cup shape. Then flatten a short rope and turn it to create a curve. Put the two pieces together and place them on his head.

7 FINISH THE DETAILS

Let him harden, then add dots to his face and chest and lines on his eyebrows with a brown marker.

3 CREATURES FROM THE GARBAGE DUMP

Trash or Treasure?

Your source of art supplies just might be as close as your garbage can. Hmmm, anything in here that you can use?

Do you know what that wooden thing is? Your grandma might. Or does your family still use them? Turn the page to see what it is and how you can use it to make art.

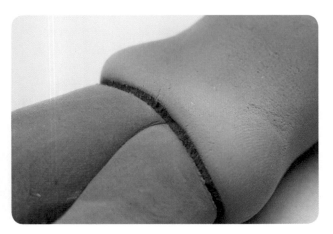

As air dry clay dries, sometimes cracks will appear. This is normal, but you can do a few things to prevent cracking.

When covering a found object with air dry clay, use a thick layer of clay so that the shrinkage of the clay isn't as noticeable. Cracks happen when the clay shrinks but the object being covered does not. When using a framework inside the clay, such as sticks or wires, use thin, strong pieces, if possible.

imagine life as a bug

MATERIALS

Black, purple, orange, white and yellow clay

Paperclips • Clothespin spring

Toothpick • Nail

Twisty tie • Spring

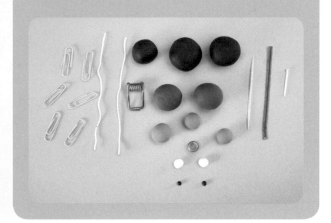

Take a break

Complicated projects, like this bug, will be easier to do if you make the body and leg parts one day and then finish the next day. That gives the body and legs time to dry firm.

Fresh, soft clay is easily pushed out of shape, which can make your project flop. That would mean a flat bug! If you get impatient to finish the project all in one sitting, consider starting two bugs. Or even more. Use your imagination to make each one different. It may take longer, but the end result will be bugs that actually stand up. How fun is that!

This bug was created with bits of this and that from around the house. You'll probably end up finding different things, and that's just fine! Terrific, in fact. There are many ways to make a bug, especially recycled bugs. But study this one to see how found objects were used. Then, use your imagination to figure out other ways that discarded things could be used in your next creation.

1 Open up the paperclips to create leg shapes. Make 2 black clay balls, then form them into two ovals. Flatten them and sandwich the legs in the middle between the two ovals. Set the body and legs upside down and let harden overnight.

2 **MAKE THE HEAD AND NECK**
For the neck, roll a small black ball. Press onto the body. Press half of a toothpick into the neck. Roll a second ball for the head.

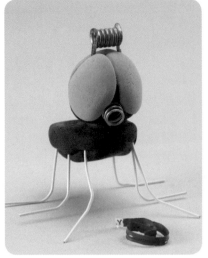

3 Place the second ball on the toothpick. Place the ends of the clothespin spring into the top of the head.

4 **FINISH THE HEAD**
Make an orange ball for the back of the head. Flatten it and press it in place. Make two orange eggs for the cheeks. Flatten them and press in place. For the mouth, press in a small spring. For the tongue, roll up a red twisty tie and press it inside the spring.

5 **ADD THE WINGS**
To make wings, make two purple egg shapes, then flatten them. Press them in place. If you want to add more color, add spots or stripes with clay or markers.

6 **ADD TAIL, ANTENNA AND EYES**
The eyes are placed on a piece of toothpick threaded through the middle of the clothespin spring. Before adding the eyes, put a bit of glue on the ends of the toothpick to help the eyes stay in place. Bend paperclips to create the antenna.

7 Finish up any last minute details, adding spots to the face and a nose.

design a robot that writes in code

This robot started as a collection of discarded hardware and found objects. In order to design your own robot, you'll need a collection of your own stuff.

What's behind your couch, under your bed or in your yard? Do you have any broken toys? Find a can or box and start collecting now. Of course it's a good idea to check with other family members to see if something belongs to them before you use it.

Next time you go for a walk, be on the lookout for tiny objects to add to your treasure box. You never know what you'll find, when you'll need it, or how it might be used!

MATERIALS

Clay in various colors • Found objects

1 GATHER YOUR TREASURE

See if any spare pieces you have lying around might be used to create a robot. If you can't find similar pieces, substitute other items. Or how about changing the design completely? Remember, there isn't a right or wrong way to do this. It needs to all stick together, but beyond that, it's up to you!

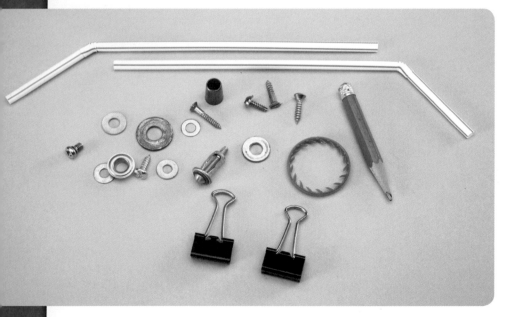

2 CREATE THE BODY

Use five pieces of clay in three colors to create the robot's body and legs. Stack the shapes with two for the legs, one for a side pocket, one for the lower half and one for the top.

3 ADD HEAD AND NECK

Use the ring leftover from a bottle to create the head. Use twist ties or string to hang hardware for his eyes. The top of a pencil makes a great nose and add a screw for the mouth. Use matching clay to attach.

Use It Again

There are many ways to use found objects with clay. Here are a few ideas:

- Create a mystery. Embed some pieces in the clay so that just part of it sticks out. See if people can guess what it is.
- Use one object to support another. Push one piece, such as a nail or a wire, into the clay. After the clay has dried, use that piece to hold up another one.
- Use clay to add height to a piece.
- Use clay to balance a piece so it sits level.

a robot that cleans your room

MATERIALS

Your favorite color of clay

Found objects, such as a straw, magnifying glass, the tab from a can, wheels, rings and an eraser.

Now we all know that this robot can't really clean up your room. But making robots like this one will help keep your room clean! Why? Because in order to make robots you'll need stuff, and in order to get stuff, you'll have to pick up little bits of this and that, stuff which used to just litter your floor and toybox and closet. So your room will get cleaner, right?

Of course, if you're like me, your stuff might start overflowing your treasure can. But that's another problem. How much stuff is too much, anyway?

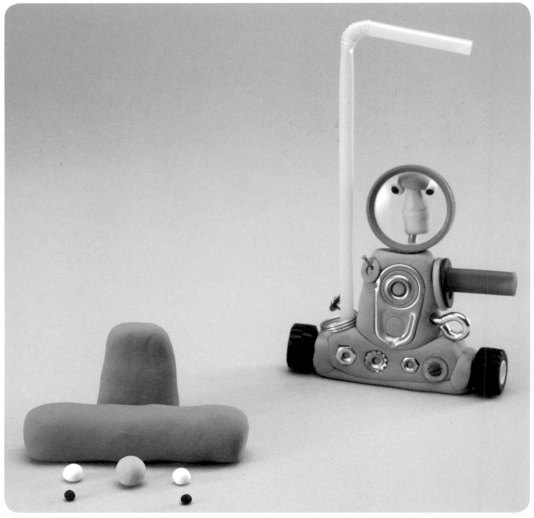

1 ASSEMBLE YOUR PIECES

In order to make a robot similar to Clean Sweep, you'll probably need to make some substitutions in materials. Look around and see what's in your room. Look for a variety of screws, straws, the tab from a can, a magnifying glass and more to add to your clay body. Stack the clay and make some eyeballs. Are there things that you found that are even better than the ones used here?

2 CREATE THE BODY AND HEAD

Put together shapes of clay to create a solid body, then embed found objects into the clay. There is no one right way to do this, just be sure that all of the pieces have enough clay to hold them in place. You may have to prop the piece as you are working so that the parts don't droop.

Make his head from a pencil eraser pressed over a big nail. The top of his head, which fits over the eraser, is a clay ball with the eyes attached.

3 You can make Clean Sweep's face plate from a magnifying glass with the handle embedded into the clay. How can a pencil eraser and a little clay look so fierce!

4 To keep the found objects from shifting position, prop your robot and let him dry overnight.

wild beast of the forest

Imagine walking through the park and seeing this creature between the trees. His legs, horns and tail are all things that are found in the yard or a garden. Do you think that you could make a whole herd of these, each one different from the one before?

This one has twigs for legs, the flower stems of a lily plant for antlers and part of another flower as a tail. Then clay and glue hold the whole thing together. You don't have to find these exact same shapes for making a beast. Just find shapes that you like, shapes that make you think of legs and antlers and hair. Just make sure that they are clean and bug free before you bring them inside!

1 CREATE THE BODY AND LIMBS

Mix together white, brown and just a bit of black clay. Leave it a bit streaky. Make an oval or short, thick rope for the body.

For legs, cut 4 sticks, all about the same length. Cut a stick for the neck. Poke holes in the body and add some glue inside. Press legs and neck into the holes.

Make a hole for the tail. To help hold the legs in a standing position, place beast in a shallow container or box. Let it sit overnight to dry.

2 MAKE THE HEAD

Create an egg shape for the head. Cut in the mouth with a plastic tool. Wiggle your tool to open the mouth. Add teeth. Close the mouth part way. Poke in holes for nostrils. Add the eyes.

To hold the head in place, prop with a wad of taped-together paper towel.

This project requires some drying time between stages in order to let the clay firm up around the sticks and hold them in place. Plan to do the body, neck, legs and tail one day. Then add the head and shaggy layers the next day. You could even break it up into 3 stages, with the head and antlers going on the second day and the shaggy mane and hair the third day. Do what works for you!

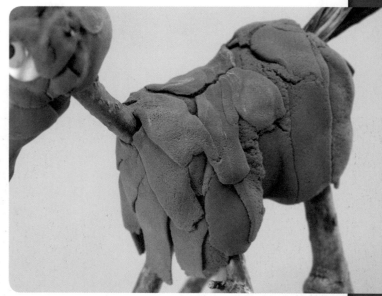

3 Cut stems that will fit for the antlers and tail. Poke holes for the antlers. Add glue to the holes. Stick in the antlers and the tail.

4 To make shaggy-looking hair, make a rope from the mixed brown clay. Flatten it. Pull the flat strips to make them look shaggy. Press some to the body. Add small pieces between the antlers and over the forehead. Keep adding more until it's covered and you're satisfied.

You may notice some cracks around the twigs, caused by the clay shrinking as it dried. I think this makes him look even more like he's a creature of the forest. What do you think? If you don't like the cracks, you can mix more clay and add more hair to cover up the cracked areas.

Once he is thoroughly dry, remove him from the container. What would you call this creature? Might he be a Dorse? Or a Helk?

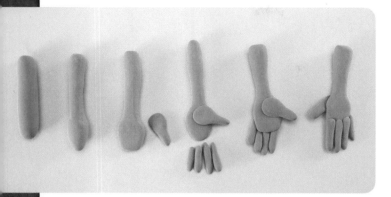

hands

Think about making hands in 3 to 5 stages. Just like with the foot, you can stop after each and say that you're done right there. Or, you can keep going and add more detail.

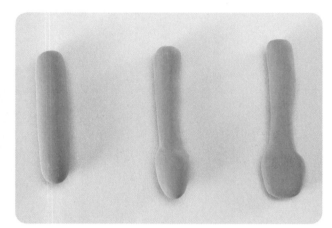

1 ROPE TO PADDLE SHAPE
Start with a rope, then roll the wrist between your fingers. Smooth out the arm. Flatten the end into a paddle shape.

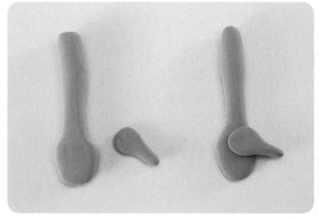

2 THUMB
To make the thumb, roll an egg shape, then stretch the small end of the egg a bit in order to create a thumb. Press this thumb to the bottom of the hand. It looks big, doesn't it? It will look smaller when the fingers are added.

3 FINISHED HAND
Roll a short rope for each finger, once again looking at your own hand to see which fingers are longer and which are shorter. Roll 4 small ropes, one for each finger. Press these ropes to the top of the hand. On the top it looks a bit funny…

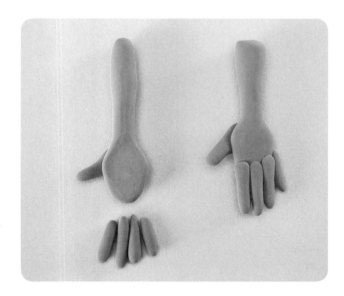

…but the palm is kind of sweet.

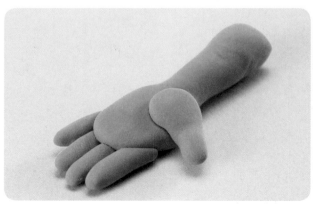

werewolf

This werewolf might be imaginary, but his teeth look real enough, don't they? He looks like he might be related to the Wild Beast of the Forest, and maybe he is. At least his hair or fur looks similar. If you have any clay left over from the wild beast project, you could use it here.

MATERIALS

1 skewer

Brown, black, white, orange and red clay

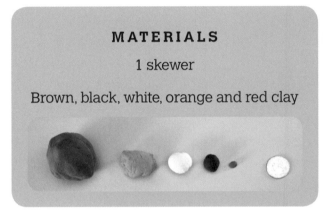

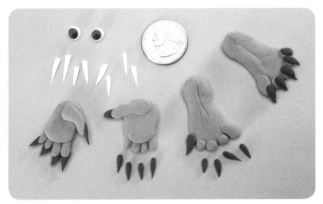

1 MAKE HANDS, FEET, TEETH AND EYES

For skin tones, mix together white and a bit of brown clay. Then add a dot of red and mix again. Make hands and feet. To make feet, refer to the Orangutan project. Make sure your werewolf's feet are big! For long, sharp fingernails and toenails, make flattened cone shapes and press to fingers and toes. From white clay, make teeth and eyeballs. Add a colored iris and black dots for pupils to the eyes. Set all aside to harden a bit.

2 FORM THE BODY

Make a chunky rope shape from brown clay. For the legs and arms, make a skinny rope for each. Cut a skewer into two 4" (10cm) pieces and one 2" (5cm) piece.

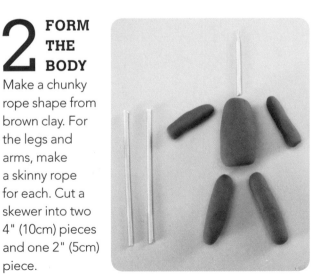

3 ATTACH LEGS

Insert a 4" (10cm) skewer into each leg, then push it into the body at an angle so the skewer goes all the way through. Poke the 2" (5cm) skewer into the neck area. Make a small ball of clay for the neck and place it over the neck skewer.

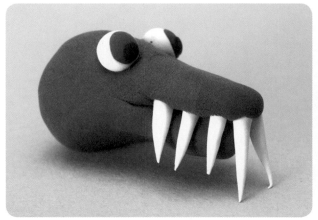

4 ATTACH ARMS AND HANDS

Bend the arms at the elbows so the werewolf can do an action pose. Press arms to the top of the body, just below neck. Press the hands at the end of the arms and press his feet to the legs. Prop him so that he stands. Support his arms so that they won't droop and let him dry overnight in that position.

5 MAKE THE HEAD

Create an egg shape. Cut open the mouth. Wiggle the tool to open the mouth wider so that there is room to add the teeth. Close the mouth. Add his eyes.

6 ATTACH THE HEAD, BEGIN SHAG

Press his head over his neckbone. From the streaky clay, make long ropes. Flatten ropes and rip off shaggy pieces. Attach scraggly fur all over the body, limbs and head.

7

Add flattened egg shapes for ears and make a black ball for the nose. Press in place. Poke in nostrils. Prop again and let dry overnight.

goblin

What makes the goblin a bit of a challenge, besides his grumpy personality and bad jokes, is that he has no fur, like a werewolf, or long wrappings, like a mummy, to cover up his body shape. If you bend the clay in places where bones don't really bend, it will show and he won't look as real. Look at your arms and legs and see where they are straight and where they bend. Try to copy those bends when you make the goblin.

MATERIALS

Green, brown, white and black clay

Stone or stick

Teeth and eyeballs made ahead of time

1 PREPARE

Gather the materials. Prepare the clay by mixing the brown, green and white clay to get a goblin shade of green.

2 MAKE BODY PARTS, BEGIN ASSEMBLING THE BODY

Make a tall, skinny egg shape for the body and press it onto the rock. Make skinny ropes for the arms and legs. Make hands and feet, with only 3 fingers and a thumb on each hand and only 4 toes on each foot. Attach his hands and feet to his arms and legs. Use a straw tool to press in fingernail and toenail shapes.

For the neck, press in a toothpick, then add a small ball of clay over it. Attach the legs under the body.

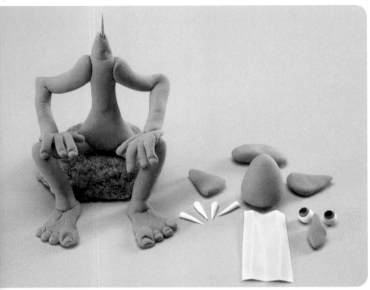

3 COMPLETE BODY ASSEMBLY

Press the arms just below the neck. Arrange the hands on the knees.

4 MAKE THE HEAD

Start with an egg and use a bent plastic tool to make his mouth wavy. Open the mouth wide and insert 4 teeth, then close. Make a long, skinny egg for the nose. Press the wide end of his nose to the middle of his face. Use your fingers to pinch the bridge of the nose to make it skinnier. To make nostrils, insert toothpick halfway up and lift.

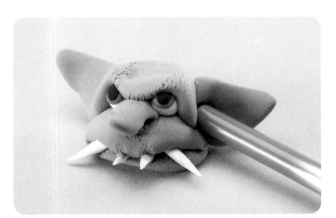

5 ADD EYES, EARS AND FOREHEAD

Press eyes right next to his nose. Add a flattened oval piece on top to create the brow and forehead. Press down on the forehead between the eyes to make him look grumpy. Make egg shapes for ears. Flatten, then press in place. Use the handle of a small paintbrush to put a hole in each ear. This also helps the ears stick to the head.

6 ADD HAIR

Place his head on his body. For hair, make long skinny ropes from black clay. Press one end of rope to the head, then cut hair by breaking it off. This makes a raggy, tousled look for the goblin.

troll

According to the stories, there are rock trolls, bridge trolls, forest trolls and cave trolls. What they have in common is that they are very strong but maybe not the swiftest beings that ever walked on two legs! This version of a troll has a little head and big feet and hands to show that he is strong, but…uh…what was I saying?

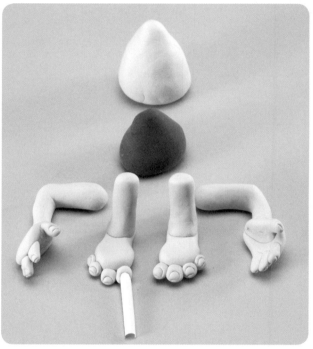

MATERIALS

White and brown clay

1 hardened clay tooth • 2 clay eyes

Brown watercolor paint

2 pieces of skewer at 4" (10cm) and a 2" (5cm) piece

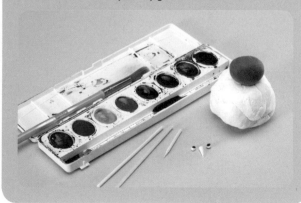

1 MAKE ARMS AND LEGS
Make ropes for the arms and legs, making sure the arms are longer than the legs. Bend the arms at the elbows.

Make hands that are wide and fat with short fingers and wide feet to match, then press in place.

Tip

If you need to prop him up while working, use a coffee cup. Lay a paper towel over the cup to keep his squishy belly from picking up marks.

2 CREATE PANTS AND BODY

Roll a short, squat egg shape with the brown clay. Put a 4" (10cm) skewer into each leg so that half of it sticks out the top. Press both exposed skewers up through the bottom of the pants so they come out the top. Stand up the legs and pants. Prop him against something so he dries in a standing position.

Make a large egg-shaped body with the white clay. To make room for the pants to fit, press your thumb into the bottom of the egg to create an indentation.

3 ASSEMBLE THE BODY

Poke the leg skewers into the body. Don't worry if a little bit of the skewers poke through the top. The head will cover them.

Poke in a belly button with a straw tool. Put in a neckbone using a short skewer. Place a little bit of glue where the arms will go and press on the arms.

4 CREATE THE HEAD

Roll a small egg shape. Cut in the mouth, opening it up so that you can add the tooth. Add a small egg for the nose. Press in the eyes. Press two holes in his nose. Press clay hair into his nostrils.

5

Set the head on his body low and further down on his chest so that he appears a bit hunched over. Add small egg shapes for his ears and small clay ropes for eyebrows. Give him a wart! Roll a tiny ball and place it on his nose. Add strips of clay for his hair. If you like, mix a little white in his hair to make him look older.

6

Let him dry, then paint the body using brown watercolor to make him look dirty. Brush with plain water to remove any extra paint. Pat dry with a paper towel.

(are you my) mummy?

Make the shape for the mummy, including the arms and legs, but don't add the fingers or toes until after he's all wrapped up. That seems appropriate for a mummy, don't you think? Sort of like floating fingers and toes.

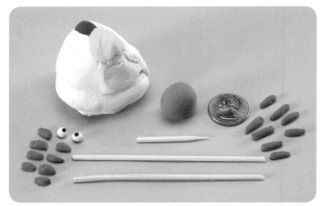

1 MIX COLOR CLAY FOR CLOTH

Mix a lot of white with a little yellow and just a touch of black and brown to make a dirty white color. Be careful to add the colors to the white clay just a bit at a time so that it doesn't get too dark. Leave the clay streaky so that it will look like moldy, dirty cloth.

2 MAKE BODY AND ARM SHAPES

The body is a short, thick rope shape. The arms are thin ropes with paddle shapes at the ends. The legs are thicker ropes. Bend the end of the rope to create an L-shape for the feet.

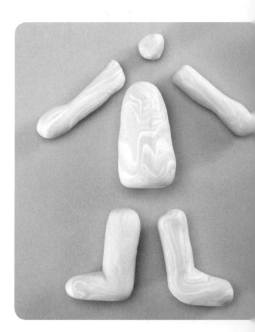

MATERIALS

White, yellow, black and brown clay

2 skewer pieces, 3 ½" (9cm) long and one shorter piece

2 hardened clay eyeballs

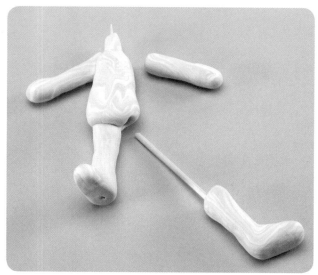

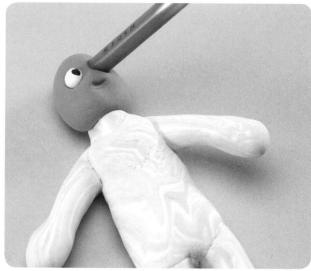

3 ASSEMBLE THE BODY

Press skewers into the legs, leaving half sticking out of the top of the legs. Press the leg skewers into the body. Make the neck by pressing in a toothpick or a piece of skewer and add a small clay ball.

4 MAKE THE HEAD

Create an egg shape. Indent the eye sockets with your finger, then press on both sides of the nose area to make it stick out a bit. Press in the eyes so that they are crooked. For the mummy wrap, roll long strips of the mixed clay. Flatten the strips so they are quite thin. Tear wrap into short strips, then wrap each strip loosely around the head.

5

For the fingers and toes, roll little balls into short rope shapes. Add fingernails if you like. Press fingers and toes in place. Position hands so that they are pointing straight out but the fingers are pointing down.

Prop him so that he dries standing up with arms pointing out.

6

Let dry overnight. Once he is dry, wrap the rest of him. Leave some pieces hanging like he's coming apart.

zombie

The tricks to making a zombie are: the sickly color of the skin and strange eyes surrounded by dark circles and straight arms. Make a whole troop of these and you can almost hear them marching, marching, marching…yikes! Back in the clay bag with them! Nice to be in control, isn't it?

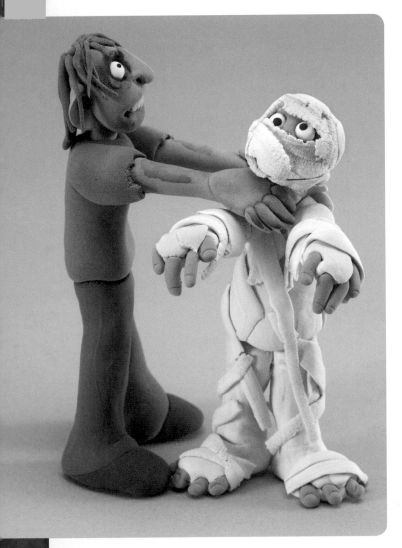

1 MIX THE SKIN COLORS
Start with white and add a bit of green, brown and yellow.

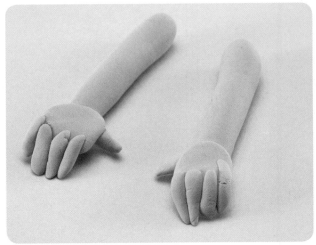

2 MAKE THE HANDS AND ARMS
Make and assemble well enough in advance that they can harden. Notice the position of the hands and fingers. Creepy!

MATERIALS

White, green, brown and yellow clay, with other colors of your choice for clothes

2 pieces each 3 ½" (9cm) skewers and 1 short piece for neck

Clay eyeballs (one plain white)

Brown watercolor paint

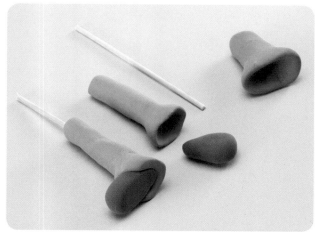

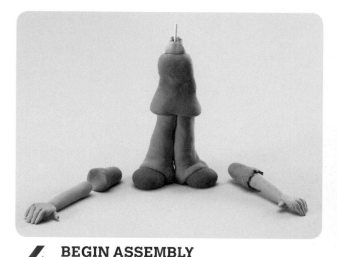

3 MAKE PANTS, SHOES AND THE SHIRT

Make the legs from two small ropes. Press your thumb into the bottom of each leg to make room for the shoe. Stick the skewers through the leg, with part sticking out at the top. Make the shoe from an egg shape and press in place. Set the legs aside to harden.

Make an egg shape for the shirt. Open it up at the bottom with your thumb. Pinch the edges to make it look like a T-shirt.

4 BEGIN ASSEMBLY

Slide the shirt down on the skewers to set over the pants. Make egg shapes for the sleeves. Open up the big end with your finger or a paintbrush handle. Pull and rip edges of sleeves. Place the arms into the sleeves. If the arm is totally dry, you might need a little glue to keep it in place. Press and glue his arms to his sides.

Add a toothpick for the neckbone. Add a small ball to create the neck.

5 START THE HEAD

Make an egg shape. Cut open the mouth, wiggling your tool to open it wide. For the teeth, insert a flat strip of white clay. Make indentations in the strip to make it look like teeth, then close the mouth a bit.

6 ADD FEATURES

For the nose, press on a long egg shape. Use a toothpick to pull up the nostrils. Use a round paintbrush handle to press in the eye sockets. Before adding the eyes, paint the sockets with watery brown watercolor paint to make him look even more zombie-like.

7 FINISH

Insert the eyes. Put the head on the body and add strips of clay for hair. Prop and let dry in a standing position, with arms out in front. When it's totally dry, add some brown watercolor wash over the whole thing to make him look dirty.

5 DINOSAURS AND DRAGONS

Dragon or Dino?

The word dinosaur comes from a Greek word meaning "terrible lizard." While neither dinosaurs or dragons are lizards, they can sure seem terrible!

Details Make Dragons Different
These dragons have the same body shape, but the colors, scales and spikes make them look very different from each other. The turquoise dragon was easier to make than the red one because he has fewer details, and his head didn't need to be propped while he dried.

Dragons Look Like Dinosaurs
Since the body shape of a dragon is so much like that of a dinosaur, learn how to make one and you'll have an idea of how to start the other.

Keep Your Teacups or Coffee Cups Handy
Because of the long necks and heavy heads, both dinosaurs and dragons benefit from a little careful propping while they dry.

triceratops

The triceratops, which is thought to have lived 65 million years ago, is estimated to have weighed more than 13,000 pounds. This tiny clay triceratops is probably ¼ the size of a real triceratop's toenails! But that doesn't mean that he can't look fierce. It must be those three horns, or maybe it's the scowl!

Make sure you prop him up while he dries so that his legs won't collapse. Splat! To keep that from happening, have some rolled up pieces of paper towel held together by tape ready to place under his belly and head.

> **MATERIALS**
>
> Green, white and black clay
>
> Clay eyes
>
> Toothpick

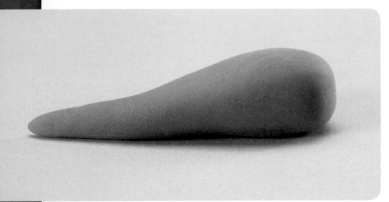

1 MAKE THE BODY

Mix this dino's color by adding a bit of black and white to green. Make an egg shape, then roll the small end into a point to create a tail.

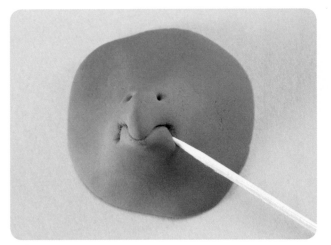

2 MAKE THE HEAD

Roll an egg shape. Press the large end of the egg onto the work surface so that it flairs out to create the flange (collar). Pinch the edges of the flange to make it slightly rippled. To make the beak-like nose, roll the small end into a point. Cut in a mouth. Open the mouth slightly, then reshape the nose with your fingers. Use a toothpick to press in and shape the corners of the mouth. Press in nostril holes.

3 Make three cones for horns and press them in place. Add the eyes. To create texture on the flange, roll tiny balls and place them around the edge.

4 MAKE THE LEGS
Roll four ropes, with the two back ones being slightly larger than the front ones. Press legs onto the body. Use a toothpick to press in lines for toes. Prop up your triceratops on a rolled up paper towel to give the legs a chance to dry.

5 PROP HIM UP TO DRY
Press in a toothpick as his neckbone and attach the head. Keep your triceratops propped until he is dry enough to stand on his own.

brachiosaurus

Remember Spike the Snake? Our brachiosaurus begins in almost the same way, except with a fatter belly. You'll roll that long body all in one piece. The trick is to figure out how to prop his neck and tail so that those graceful curves stay in place. Add four legs, and you have a miniature Brachiosaurus.

MATERIALS

Gray, brown and white clay

Clay eyes

Toothpick

1 PREPARE THE MATERIALS
Mix gray and brown clays to create your color.

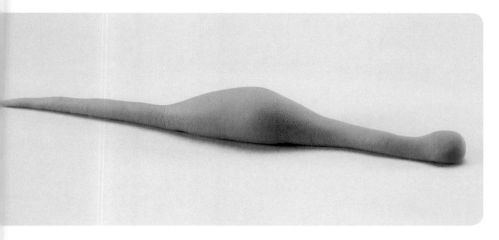

2 CREATE THE BODY

For the body, neck and tail, roll a large ball, then turn it into a drumstick shape. Roll the large end of the drumstick into a long pointed tail. Roll and stretch the small end of the drumstick to create a long neck.

Leave a small ball shape at the end for the head. At this point, the whole thing should like a snake that swallowed a ball.

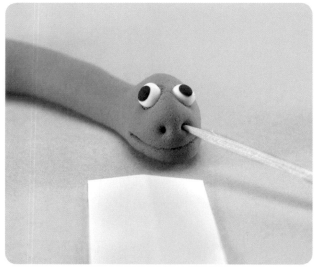

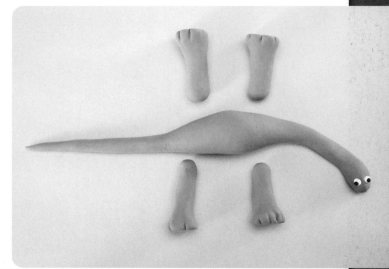

3 CREATE THE FACE

Cut in the mouth. Add eyes. Poke two holes for the nostrils.

4 MAKE THE LEGS

Have your support pieces ready. Make four ropes all the same size. Use a toothpick to press lines in to make the toes. Press the legs onto his body.

5 PROP HIM UP TO DRY

Set him up how you'd like him. Prop him well, then let him dry in that position.

red dragon

MATERIALS

Red clay • Toothpick

Straw tool • Brush handle

With his long, thin body and facial whiskers, this guy looks like he comes from the Far East! Notice the lack of wings? Dragons shown in Chinese art often don't have wings, while ones pictured in European art usually do. What they have in common is a reputation for being powerful creatures.

As with all your projects, make the eyes and teeth in advance. While you're at it, make some long twisty whiskers, too. Set them aside to harden.

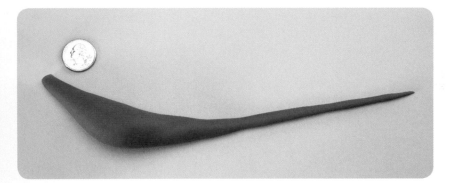

1 MAKE THE BODY
Make a long football shape. Stretch and roll one end of the football into a long tail. Roll and stretch the other end to make the neck. Press a piece of toothpick into the neck of the body that will hold the head.

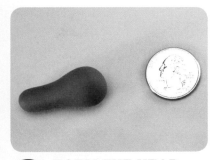
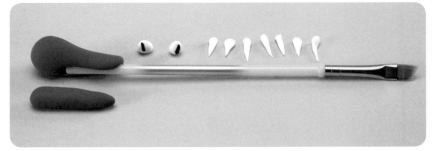

2 FORM THE HEAD
Make a small drumstick shape. Press the small end of the drumstick over the handle of a brush. Create a separate piece for the jaw. While still on the brush, connect the two pieces. Take the head off the brush.

3 Add the teeth and then close up the mouth.

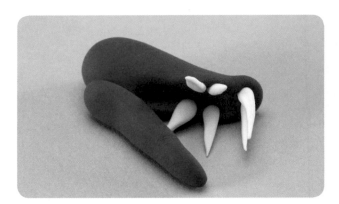

4 MAKE THE FACE

Add the eyes and a ball for each nostril. Poke holes in each nostril, then press the head onto the toothpick.

5 MAKE SCALES

Use a rounded straw tool to cut in scales. To create ripples on his chestplate, rock a toothpick across the front.

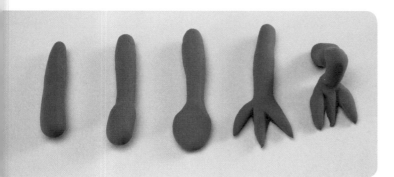

6 MAKE THE LEGS

Make 4 ropes for legs. Make front and back feet the same. Roll each into an egg, then a drumstick. Press the small ends to flatten the feet. Cut in toes. Roll toes between your fingers to make them long and skinny. Don't stretch them or they'll break off! Do a quick turn in the center of each for knees and elbows.

7 FINISH YOUR DRAGON

Make cones for spikes. Press spikes along the spine and on the head. Add any final decorations to polish him off.

how to fix your dragon

Yes, sometimes pieces do break or crack. If this happens, try one of these tricks:

Glue pieces back together with clear glue. Then add another clay scale or spike or piece of hair to cover the damaged area.

Rip off the broken piece. Make another one just like it and replace the broken one. Add glue to help it stick.

how to make clay wings

Because air dry clay can be quite fragile, wings that are made out of clay need to be quite thick.

1 ADD HOLES FOR THE WINGS

When making the dragon, use a toothpick to add a hole where each wing will fit.

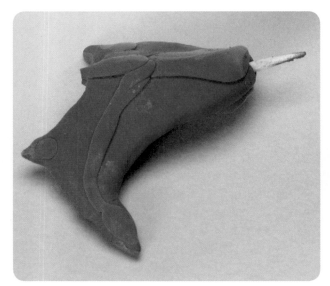

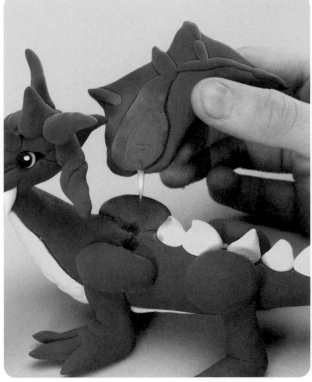

2 MAKE THE WING

Flatten and shape matching clay into a wing shape.

3

Press a flat toothpick into the wing, leaving enough toothpick exposed to allow you to poke the wings into the body.

5

Let the wings dry until firm and then press them into the holes in the dragon.

4

Decorate wings with clay lines, dots or add color with markers.

how to make paper wings

Paper wings are lighter, thinner and more delicate than the clay ones. Flip the pattern to make the other wing.

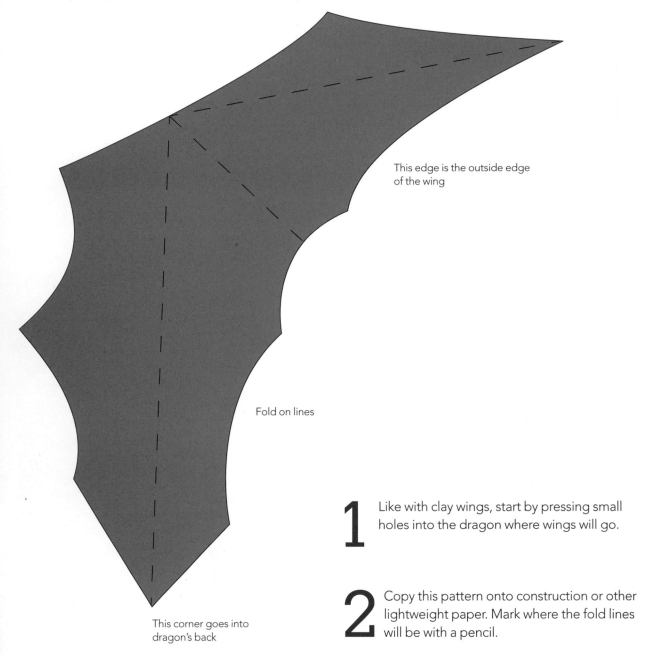

This edge is the outside edge of the wing

Fold on lines

This corner goes into dragon's back

1 Like with clay wings, start by pressing small holes into the dragon where wings will go.

2 Copy this pattern onto construction or other lightweight paper. Mark where the fold lines will be with a pencil.

3 Color or paint wings if you like, let them dry and poke the corner into the hole you made.

4 Use a dull knife and a ruler to draw along the fold lines to create a slight impression in the wings.

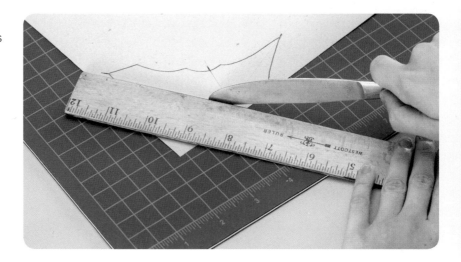

5 Cut out and fold the wings on the scored lines. Press the pointed end of paper wings into holes in the dragon.

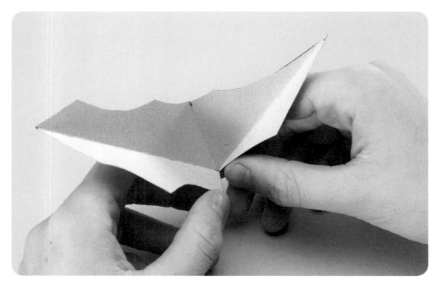

About the Author

Bored? What's that?

Maureen Carlson remembers that her mother, AnaBel Peck, never let her say, "I'm bored!" According to AnaBel, being bored meant you weren't being creative about the way you used your time. "Nothing to do? How could that be?" There were always art supplies around, and of course there were books and pets and all of the outdoors to explore. If that failed, there were dishes to wash! Or gardens to weed! Or corners to dust.

Thanks to that early training, Maureen says that she can always find something to do and never seems to find time to do all of the things on her lists, which, of course, are always expanding. And she feels very lucky about that!

Maureen is an author, teacher, Storyclay Teller, artist and retreat facilitator. Her previous books with F+W Media, Inc. include *How to Make Clay Characters* and *Clay Characters for Kids*, both published by North Light Books. In 1998 she and husband, Dan, opened Maureen Carlson's Center for Creative Arts in Jordan, Minnesota.

For more info, see WeeFolk.com or MaureenCarlson.com.

Metric Conversion Chart

To convert	to	multiply by
Inches	Centimeters	2.54
Centimeters	Inches	0.4
Feet	Centimeters	30.5
Centimeters	Feet	0.03
Yards	Meters	0.9
Meters	Yards	1.1

Crazy Clay Creatures. Copyright © 2013 by Maureen Carlson. Manufactured in China. All rights reserved. No part of this book may be reproduced in any form or by any electronic or mechanical means including information storage and retrieval systems without permission in writing from the publisher, except by a reviewer who may quote brief passages in a review. Published by IMPACT Books, an imprint of F+W Media, Inc., 10151 Carver Road, Suite 200, Blue Ash, OH 45242. (800) 289-0963. First Edition.

 Other fine IMPACT Books are available from your favorite bookstore, art supply store or online supplier. Visit our website at fwmedia.com.

17 16 15 14 13   5 4 3 2 1

ISBN-13: 978-1-4403-2221-1

DISTRIBUTED IN CANADA BY FRASER DIRECT
100 Armstrong Avenue
Georgetown, ON, Canada L7G 5S4
Tel: (905) 877-4411

DISTRIBUTED IN THE U.K. AND EUROPE
BY F&W MEDIA INTERNATIONAL, LTD
Brunel House, Forde Close, Newton Abbot, TQ12 4PU, UK
Tel: (+44) 1626 323200, Fax: (+44) 1626 323319
Email: enquiries@fwmedia.com

DISTRIBUTED IN AUSTRALIA BY CAPRICORN LINK
P.O. Box 704, S. Windsor NSW, 2756 Australia
Tel: 02 4560 1600, Fax: 02 4577 5288
Email: books@capricornlink.com.au

Edited by Vanessa Wieland
Designed by Wendy Dunning and Kelly O'Dell
Photography by Christine Polomsky
Production coordinated by Mark Griffin
Hand modeling by Ian Barker

Acknowledgments

How many people does it really take to create a book like this? Even though I've been writing how-to books since 1991, I didn't even BEGIN to understand how many individual talents were involved until I went to the F+W offices to do the photo shoot for this book. Thank you ALL!

A special bow to Vanessa Wieland, editor, and Christine Polomsky, photographer, who turned what could have been a stressful week into one that was thoroughly joyful. And a round of applause for the hand model, Ian, age 11, who hung in there for a long day of hand shots. Bravo!

Meanwhile, back at the Center for Creative Arts, it was Renee Carlson who picked up the slack and saw that things did, indeed get done. You did a great job making the Human Beans, Chess Set and Troops! Blessings.

Dedication

For Dan, who encourages me to follow through with my dreams.

For Ian and Gideon Boyer, without whom I never would have attempted a book for boys. And I had so much fun doing it!

Ideas. Instruction. Inspiration.

Download FREE bonus materials at impact-books.com/airdry-clay.

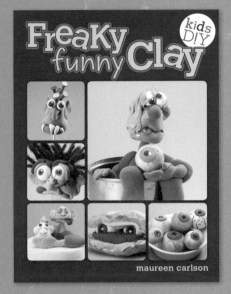

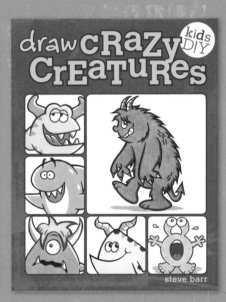

IMPACT-BOOKS.COM

- ▶ Connect with your favorite artists
- ▶ Get the latest in comic, fantasy and sci-fi art instruction, tips and techniques
- ▶ Be the first to get special deals on the products you need to improve your art

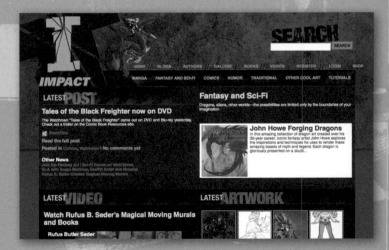